Theory Paper Grade 1   2015   A
Model Answers

1   (10)

(a)

(b)

2   *There are many ways of completing this question. The specimen completion below would receive full marks.*   (10)

3   (10)

(a)   A G F E D B♭ C A F

(b)

4   (10)

   ff   *f*   *mf*   *mp*   *p*   *pp*

5 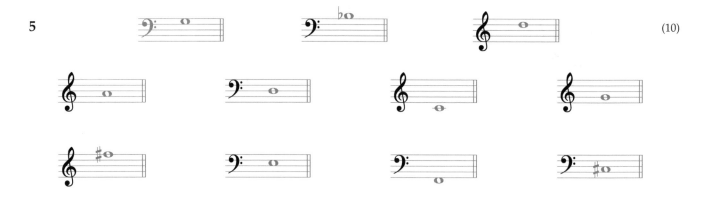 (10)

6  (10)

7 (10)

(a)

(b)

8 (a) at a walking pace / medium speed (10)
moderate speed / moderately
quiet / soft
in a singing style
getting louder / gradually getting louder

(b) (10)

(i) 3rd
(ii) *There are two possible answers to this question. Either of the answers shown would receive full marks.*

(iii) semiquaver / 16th note
(iv) 4; 5
(v) three

(c)  (10)

2·75

ABRSM

Grade
1

Music Theory Past Papers 2015

Model Answers

ABRSM Grade 1

Welcome to ABRSM's *Music Theory Past Papers 2015 Model Answers*, Grade 1. These answers are a useful resource for students and teachers preparing for ABRSM theory exams and should be used alongside the relevant published theory past papers.

All the answers in this booklet would receive full marks but not all possible answers have been included for practicable reasons. In these cases other reasonable alternatives may also be awarded full marks. For composition-style questions (where candidates must complete a rhythm, compose a melody based on a given opening or set text to music) only one example of the many possible answers is given.

For more information on how theory papers are marked and some general advice on taking theory exams, please refer to the Music Theory Grade 1 web page: www.abrsm.org/theory1.

Using these answers

- Answers are given in the same order and, where possible, in the same layout as in the exam papers, making it easy to match answer to question.

- Where it is necessary to show the answer on a stave, the original stave is printed in grey with the answer shown in black, for example:

- Alternative answers are separated by an oblique stroke (/) or by *or*, for example:

getting slower / gradually getting slower

- The old-style crotchet rest 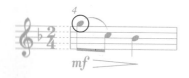 is accepted as a valid alternative to the modern symbol .

- Answers that require the candidate to write out a scale or chord have been shown at one octave only. Reasonable alternatives at different octaves can also receive full marks.

- Sometimes the clef, key and time signature of the relevant bar(s) are included for added clarity, for example:

© 2016 by The Associated Board of the Royal Schools of Music
Published by ABRSM (Publishing) Ltd, a wholly owned subsidiary of ABRSM
Cover by Kate Benjamin & Andy Potts
Printed in England by Halstan & Co. Ltd, Amersham, Bucks

Theory Paper Grade 1   2015   B
Model Answers

1   (10)

2   *There are many ways of completing this question. The specimen completion below would receive full marks.*   (10)

3   (10)

4   (10)

5   (10)

(a)   2nd   4th   2nd   1st /   3rd   6th   7th   5th   8th /
8th / 8ve   8ve / 1st

(b)   three

6   (10)

(a)

(b)   C E G   G B D

7   5th   8th / 8ve   4th   (10)
       7th   3rd   6th

8   (a)   fairly quick / quite quick / quick, but not as quick as Allegro   (10)
             quiet / soft
             getting quieter / gradually getting quieter
             play the notes detached / jumpy / staccato
             play the notes smoothly / slur

       (b)   (10)

             (i)   *There are six possible answers to this question. Any of the answers shown would receive full marks.*

             (ii)   semiquaver / 16th note
             (iii) 8 / last bar
             (iv)   *There are two possible answers to this question. Either of the answers shown would receive full marks.*

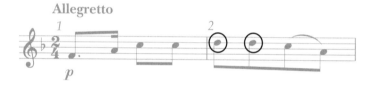

             (v)   two

       (c)   (10)

Theory Paper Grade 1   2015   C
Model Answers

1 (10)

2 *There are many ways of completing this question. The specimen completion below would receive full marks.* (10)

3 (10)

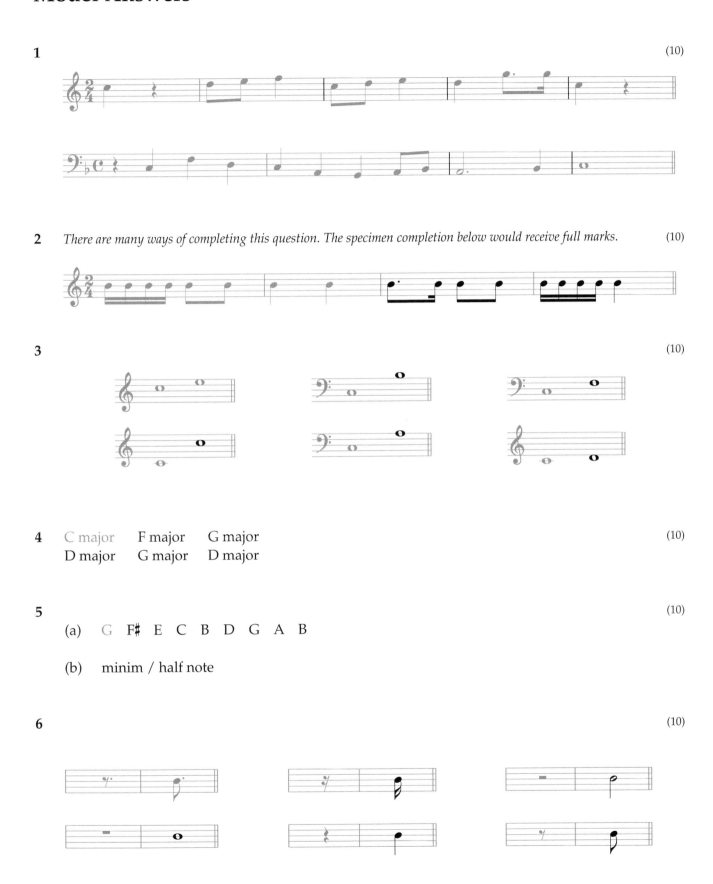

4   C major   F major   G major   (10)
   D major   G major   D major

5 (10)

(a)   G F♯ E C B D G A B

(b)   minim / half note

6 (10)

7

8 (a) fast / quick / cheerful / lively
124 crotchets in a minute / 124 quarter notes in a minute /
124 crotchet beats in a minute / 124 quarter-note beats in a minute
moderately quiet / moderately soft / medium quiet / medium soft
getting louder / gradually getting louder
loud

(b)
(i)   2
(ii)   4th
(iii) 3
(iv)   true
(v)   eight

(c)

Theory Paper Grade 1   2015   S
Model Answers

1
(a)

(b)

2 *There are many ways of completing this question. The specimen completion below would receive full marks.* (10)

3 (10)

4 (10)

(a) D B D G A C E F♯ G

(b) quaver / eighth note

5 (10)

6 7th   4th   2nd (10)
8th / 8ve 3rd   5th

7 C major   F major   G major (10)
D major   C major   D major

8 (a) fairly quick / quite quick / quick, but not as quick as Allegro (10)
moderate speed / moderately
112 crotchets in a minute / 112 quarter notes in a minute /
    112 crotchet beats in a minute / 112 quarter-note beats in a minute
moderately loud / medium loud
getting slower / gradually getting slower

(b) (10)
(i) 3; 4
(ii) C / middle C
(iii)   *staccato* (detached)
(iv) six
(v) true

(c)

Allegretto moderato ♩ = 112

(10)

Music Theory Past Papers 2015 Model Answers

Model answers for four past papers from ABRSM's 2015 Theory exams for Grade 1

Key features:

- a list of correct answers where appropriate
- a selection of likely options where the answer can be expressed in a variety of ways
- a single exemplar where a composition-style answer is required

Support material for ABRSM Theory exams

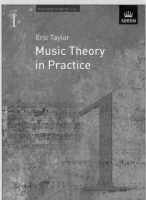

ABRSM
24 Portland Place
London W1B 1LU
United Kingdom

www.abrsm.org

ABRSM is the exam board of the Royal Schools of Music. We are committed to actively supporting high-quality music-making, learning and development throughout the world, and to producing the best possible resources for music teachers and students.

ISBN 978-1-84849-747-4

9 781848 497474